THE SCIENCE OF

SOIL

Soil for Building Materials

REBECCA
STEFOFF

Cavendish
Square

New York

Published in 2017 by Cavendish Square Publishing, LLC
243 5th Avenue, Suite 136, New York, NY 10016

Library of Congress Cataloging-in-Publication Data

Names: Stefoff, Rebecca, 1951-
Title: Soil for building materials / Rebecca Stefoff.
Description: New York : Cavendish Square Publishing, [2017] | Series: The science of soil | Includes bibliographical references and index.
Identifiers: LCCN 2016026963 (print) | LCCN 2016027397 (ebook) | ISBN 9781502621641 (library bound) | ISBN 9781502621658 (E-book)
Subjects: LCSH: Soil mechanics--Juvenile literature. | Building materials--Juvenile literature.
Classification: LCC TA455.S6 S74 2017 (print) | LCC TA455.S6 (ebook) | DDC 624.1/891--dc23
LC record available at https://lccn.loc.gov/2016026963

Editorial Director: David McNamara
Editor: Fletcher Doyle
Copy Editor: Rebecca Rohan
Associate Art Director: Amy Greenan
Designer: Stephanie Flecha
Production Coordinator: Karol Szymczuk
Photo Research: J8 Media

The photographs in this book are used by permission and through the courtesy of:
Cover Danita Delimont/Getty Images; Back cover, and used throughout the book Sinelev/Shutterstock.com; 4 Christian Aslund/Getty Images; p. 7 Antonov Roman/Shutterstock.com; p. 8 Luca Galuzzi/File:USA 10654 Bryce Canyon Luca Galuzzi 2007.jpg/Wikimedia Commons; p. 11 Meier&Poehlmann/File:Cave houses shanxi 3.jpg/Wikimedia Commons; p. 12 Sascha Grabow/Getty Images; p. 14 photogal/Shutterstock.com; p. 17 steve estvanik/Shutterstock.com; p. 18 Exonie/File:Pletenarka 2, Bozhenitsa, Bulgaria.JPG/Wikimedia Commons; p. 19 Arthur Rothstein/Library of Congress; p. 22 Sovfoto/UIG/Getty Images; p. 25 Werner Forman/Universal Images Group/Getty Images; p. 29 Sorin Colac/Shutterstock.com; p. 30 Something12356789/File:2008 competition sandcastle.jpg/Wikimedia Commons; p. 31 Becris/Shutterstock.com; p. 33 Sean Sprague/Alamy Stock Photo; p. 35 Jean-Erick PASQUIER/Gamma-Rapho/Getty Images; p. 36 Aleks Kend/Shutterstock.com; p. 39 Ernst Kucklich/Getty Images; p. 41 GABRIEL BOUYS/AFP/Getty Images.

Printed in the United States of America

Contents

Some new houses built mostly of earth are called earthships.

1 Under Foot

People started making buildings tens of thousands of years ago. To meet their need for shelter, they built houses. They also built places for work and worship.

One of the first materials people used for building is earth, or **soil**. Sometimes, they made whole buildings out of soil. At other times, they used soil in the making of other building materials, such as brick, **adobe**, **mortar**, and **concrete**. Even glass is made of sand, which is a kind of soil.

One way that people put roofs over their heads was by using the earth under their feet. Builders today still use soil as a building material. But where does soil come from?

From Rock to Soil

Soil is a blend of five things:

1. Tiny bits of earth, like sand or rock dust
2. Water
3. Gases, like the gases nitrogen and oxygen that are in the air
4. Dead and decaying things that were once alive, such as fallen leaves or pine needles, and
5. Small living things, such as bacteria and fungi

Different kinds of rock grains make different kinds of soil. The kind of soil also depends on how much water, gas, and other things it holds. But all soil is based on particles, or tiny pieces, of earth.

Those particles start out as solid rock. Over time, rock gets weathered. Wind and rain make slow but steady changes to the rock. So does flowing water, such as rivers. Particles are worn away in the form of sand or dust. This is called **erosion**.

Soil has many layers. Topsoil, the dark, moist upper layer, is where plants grow.

Heat and cold also weather the rock. Cracks form, and then chunks of stone fall free. In time, these chunks are broken down into smaller pieces, such as pebbles and gravel. Even pebbles and gravel are weathered into grains of sand and dust in time.

Erosion happens faster to some rocks than to others. Sandstone is a kind of rock that erodes easily. Granite is a

Erosion carved towers called hoodoos in Bryce Canyon, Utah.

kind of rock that holds up longer against **weathering**. The difference between these two kinds of rock is explained by **geology**, the study of the materials that make up the earth.

Sandstone is made up of many layers of sand or soil that built up over a long time, usually at the bottom of an ocean or lake. Water trickled through these layers, making a thick mixture like wet **cement**. The weight of the water then pressed the layers together to form sandstone—a "soft rock" that is easy to carve.

Granite is harder. This type of rock started out as lava, or melted rock, from volcanoes. As the lava cooled, it hardened back into rock. The melting and cooling made the new rock even harder than it was before. That is why granite breaks down into soil grains more slowly than sandstone does.

How Soil Moves

Soil forms when rock grains are mixed with water, air, and small life forms (or things that were once alive). Once soil forms, it does not always stay in place. Soil is constantly being moved around on the surface of Earth.

The same forces that break down rock into soil particles also move the soil around. Two powerful ones are wind and water. If you've ever stood on a patch of dry, dusty ground on a windy day, you may have seen wind pick up earth and blow it around. Sometimes the wind blows dirt or dust into swirling shapes like tiny tornadoes. These are called dust devils.

Houses from Wind

A vast area in northern China is called the Loess Plateau. This mostly flat area is covered with a deep layer of loess, a special kind of soil.

Loess is fine, dry soil that has been moved to its current place from the place where it formed. Rivers and glaciers move some loess. Most loess, though, is blown on the wind. The loess in China started out in the desert regions to the north and west of the Loess Plateau. Over hundreds of thousands of years, the wind carried it to the plateau, grain by grain.

In time, loess packs down into a hard mass. On the Loess Plateau, it is more than 300 feet (90 meters) thick in places. For more than a thousand years, this layer of loess has been home to millions of people.

Homes called *yaodongs* are carved into loess cliffs, or into the sides of pits dug into the loess. Whole villages and towns are made up of yaodongs. Each region of the

Millions of people live in houses carved into the earth in northern China.

Loess Plateau has its own style of yaodong. Some have gardens or crops growing on their roofs.

Living in loess makes sense. Trees are scarce on the Loess Plateau. It is hard and costly to build with wood. Loess homes also are mostly underground, so they stay warm in the winter and cool in the summer.

Yaodongs are easily damaged by earthquakes. Many people have died when their loess houses collapsed. Loess is also easily carried away by wind and water. Goats and other animals have eaten much of the grass that once covered the Loess Plateau. Without the grass to hold it in place, the soil erodes. China is working to restore the grass so that the loess—and the yaodongs—will not be lost.

Wind sometimes creates much bigger clouds of moving particles. These are called dust storms or sandstorms. One famous example is a dust storm that swept across part of the Great Plains of the United States on April 14, 1935. It is known as the Black Sunday storm because it happened on a Sunday. The cloud of dust was so thick that it blotted out the sun. People called it "the black blizzard."

Sandstorms, such as this one approaching Australia, can tower hundreds of feet into the air and travel at great speeds.

Soil, dust, and **sand** can travel for long distances on the wind. Each year, about 40 million tons (36.3 milion metric tons) of dust are carried from the Sahara Desert in North Africa all the way across the Atlantic Ocean. The dust falls on the Amazon rainforest. Heavy tropical rains wash important minerals out of the soil of the Amazon, but the African dust adds those minerals back into the soil.

Water also moves huge amounts of soil. The Mississippi River flows south through the center of the United States. Along the way, it picks up tons of earth. On the coast of Louisiana, the river empties into the Gulf of Mexico, where it leaves the soil it has carried. The river carries so much soil that the coast has moved 15 to 50 miles (24 to 80 kilometers) south over the past five thousand years.

People move soil, too—on a much smaller scale. In all parts of the world, people have taken earth from the ground and turned it into houses and other buildings.

Taos Pueblo in New Mexico may have had people living in it longer than any other North American building.

2 Earth Buildings Around the World

In a valley in New Mexico, two large buildings stand on the banks of a small river. They are reddish-brown, the same color as the earth around them. The tallest parts of the buildings are five stories high.

Each building is made up of many homes that are built side-by-side, or on top of each other. Some homes have modern windows and doors. Most of them, though, look just the way they did when they were built—between six hundred and one thousand years ago. This is Taos Pueblo. It is home to Native Americans who speak the Tiwa language. Some experts think people have lived without a break in Taos Pueblo longer than in any other building in North America.

Taos Pueblo matches the earth around it because it was built with that earth. Its thick walls are made of adobe, which is soil mixed with water and straw. Its roofs are made of a few big logs, with many smaller branches laid across them. A layer of earth is packed on top of each roof.

Adobe is one of the oldest known building materials. Sometimes called **mud** brick, it has been used in many parts of the world.

People have used soil for building in other ways, too. Some buildings are made of earth that has been taken out of the ground. Other buildings are dug into the soil itself.

Buildings Made of Earth

Sun-dried mud or adobe buildings are found in all parts of the world—except Antarctica! They come in many shapes and styles. Houses, apartment buildings, churches, schools, walls, and forts have all been built out of mud.

In the town of Harran, Turkey, people have built mud up into domes like big beehives or igloos. These houses are linked together by mud walls. In Afghanistan, square mud-walled houses with flat roofs look like flights of stairsteps on the sides of hills. In Brazil, livestock herders build small mud huts for shelter while they are away from home tending their animals.

Many builders mix mud with straw or grass, **clay**, pebbles or gravel, or even animal dung to hold it together

The mud houses of Harran, Turkey, are domed like large beehives..

Small sticks are visible inside the walls of an old wattle-and-daub building where the mud has fallen away.

and make it stronger. This type of building material is sometimes called **cob**. Hundreds of years ago, people in England and France built cob walls around their fields.

Some of these walls still stand because they have "roofs" of thick straw to protect them from rain.

Another way of building with mud is to make a framework of sticks or poles, then cover the framework with mud. This is called **wattle-and-daub** building. The frame is the wattle, and the mud is the daub. People in Africa and Europe have built this way for centuries. Some Native Americans also made wattle-and-daub structures.

Settlers on the prairies cut sod into blocks to build their houses..

Rammed-earth building also starts with a wooden frame. Unlike the wattle, though, the frame will be taken away when the building is finished. A rammed-earth frame is two walls or sheets of wood, close together but with some space between them. Builders fill up this space with earth. Every so often, they press down on the earth from above with heavy stones or wooden tools. This rams the earth together until it is solid and hard. Once the earth walls are completely dry, the wooden frame is taken away to be used again.

The oldest known rammed-earth buildings are in China. The same type of building was used for walls—including parts of the Great Wall of China. From Asia, rammed-earth building spread to Africa and Europe. Cities in Germany have rammed-earth buildings that are still in use after several hundred years.

Another way to build with earth is to use **sod** or turf. Strips or squares of soil are cut from the ground with the grass and roots still in place. Pioneers on the American prairies roofed their houses with sod. This saved wood, and the "living roofs" kept houses cool in summer and warm in winter. Sod houses can still be seen in Iceland, Sweden, Russia, and other northern countries.

Building with Brick and Concrete

Mud and adobe don't have to be piled up on the spot to make a building. They can be made into blocks, called bricks, and then taken anywhere.

By eight thousand or even ten thousand years ago, people in the Middle East were making bricks. They filled wooden squares called forms with mud, then let the mud dry in the sun. Sand and straw could be added to make sun-dried bricks stronger.

Between seven thousand and five thousand years ago, people in different parts of the world discovered that firing bricks, or baking them in ovens, made them hard, long-lasting, and waterproof. Fired bricks are made without straw.

The Oldest Bricks in China

A discovery in 2009 showed that people in China have been making bricks for much longer than anyone knew.

Workers in northwest China were digging for a new highway. They found the remains of ancient, buried buildings. Work on the highway stopped so that scientists could study the remains.

Scientists are studying ancient bricks that have opened a new window into China's long history of building with earth materials.

The scientists found houses, ash pits, and furnaces that were used for baking clay into pottery or bricks. The ash pits were a lucky find. Ancient people threw their garbage and trash into the pits. Items from the pits show what people ate and how they lived.

Among other things, the pits contained parts of five bricks—three red ones and two gray ones. All five had been heated or baked to harden them. The most exciting part of the discovery was the age of the bricks. Experts believe they are between five thousand and seven thousand years old.

Before this discovery, the oldest known bricks in China were less than five thousand years old. The five broken bricks prove that brickmaking in China started much earlier than that—maybe two thousand years earlier.

Brick structures are held together by a thick paste called mortar. It is spread between each brick. It dries hard and sticks to the bricks, forming them into solid walls. Early mortar was made of mud mixed with ash or powdered stone. Today, it is made of cement, which is a powder of dried clay along with crushed limestone that has been burned or baked. When water is added, cement turns into a thick paste that dries hard.

Many large, old structures around the world are made of brick. More than two thousand brick temples in Pagan, Burma, have stood for nine hundred years. Malbork, a castle built in Poland in the fourteenth century, is a masterpiece of brickwork. The sprawling sewer network built under London in the nineteenth century has brick walls.

Concrete is another soil-based building material. It is a blend of particles such as gravel and sand that is mixed with water and cement.

Third-century Romans used concrete to build the Baths of Caracalla.

The ancient Romans mastered the use of concrete. They added ash from volcanoes to help bind the particles together. The ash also made the concrete somewhat waterproof.

For seven hundred years, the Romans built walls, domes, and arches using concrete. Today, concrete is one of the most common building materials in the world. It is used for everything from skyscrapers to dams to superhighways. It is also made into blocks, like bricks.

Buildings in the Soil

Some buildings are made not *of* soil but *in* it. Native Americans in the Southwest built pit houses. These were rooms dug into the ground, with roofs of logs that were covered with sticks, straw, and adobe. Underground chambers called kivas were much larger. They were used for important ceremonies.

People in northern Europe built pit houses, too. These were usually roofed with sod. In hilly places, people dug the houses into the sides of hills. The only wood they needed was for doors.

For as long as people have been building, they have used soil as a building material. Over the centuries, they learned that there are many kinds of soil. Each has its own uses for building.

This tower in the Italian city of Siena is among the tallest brick buildings ever built, at 289 feet (88 meters).

3 Using Soil to Build

Soil comes in many, many varieties. To build with earth, people have to know something about the different kinds of soil. They also have to know how they can change soil, or add things to it, to make it into a better building material.

Kinds of Soil

There are three main kinds of soil. They are sand, **silt**, and clay. Each has physical features that set it apart from the others.

Sand has larger grains than silt and clay. Water drains through it easily. Sand is poor at storing the kinds of minerals and other nutrients that plants need. It contains less material from living or once-living things than other kinds of soil.

Sand is not very compactable. That means that it does not stick together well. If you squeeze a handful of dry sand, it will flow apart as soon as you relax your hand. Wet sand will stick together, but only while it is wet. This is why sand castles built on beaches don't last very long.

Silt grains are smaller than sand grains. Silt is better at holding water and plant nutrients than sand, and

it is more compactable. However, silt is eroded by wind and water more easily than any other kind of soil.

Clay has the smallest grains of any soil type.

Sand castles can be large and complex, but only as long as the sand is damp.

Combinations of silt, clay, and sand make different kinds of soil.

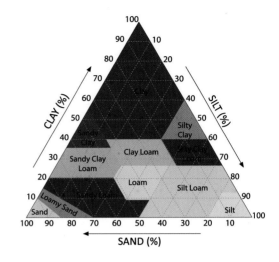

It holds onto water for a long time, and it is good at storing plant nutrients. Air does not get into clay easily, however. Clay is the most compactable kind of soil. When it is wet, it can be very sticky, and it is the easiest kind of soil to press into forms that hold their shape.

Most soil is a combination of two of the basic soil types, or all three. Soil that has a balance of all three basic types is called loam. Other mixed soils have more clay, silt, or sand in their blend. For example, clay that has sand or silt mixed in is called sandy clay or silty clay. Soil that has silt, sand, and a lot of clay is called clay loam.

Make Your Own Mud Bricks

Some of the world's oldest buildings are made of mud bricks. You can use this age-old method to make bricks for a building project of your own.

How will you dry your bricks? They can dry in any warm, dry place, such as a sunny yard or windowsill. This may take days. For faster drying, bake them in an oven, but be sure you have an adult to help you. Bake your bricks at a low temperature (250 degrees Fahrenheit or 120 degrees Celsius) for an hour or two.

Once you know how you will dry your bricks, choose the frame you'll fill with wet mud. If you are going to air-dry the bricks, you can use almost anything: sturdy cardboard boxes, the bottoms of plastic milk or juice jugs, an ice cube tray, or a tray for baking cupcakes and muffins. If you are going to use an oven, make sure that your frame can be safely baked.

Children in some regions make bricks of mud for homebuilding.

Next, mix your ingredients. Start with a large bucket or bowl of soil. Can you squeeze a handful of the soil into a ball? Does the ball hold its shape afterward? If so, the soil has some clay. It should make good bricks. Sift through the soil to remove any stones; these can weaken the bricks.

Slowly mix a trickle of water with the soil. You want mud, but it should be thick, not runny. If it feels soft and slippery, add a little sand. Adding some cut-up grass or dried plants helps hold bricks together, too.

Dry your bricks, then gently take them out of their frames. Now you are ready to build with earth.

The Best Soil for Building

What is the best kind of soil for building? The answer depends on what you want to build. The best soil for building with mud has a lot of clay in it.

The simplest way to build with soil is to pile up walls of mud, a little at a time, waiting for each layer to dry before adding another layer. This can take a long time. Also, buildings made of mud alone are not very sturdy. Water can quickly damage them or even wash them away. Many mud buildings have roofs of wood, straw, or leaves to protect the walls from rain.

Mud or adobe structures are usually coated with plaster, a paste that contains cement, lime, or ash. The plaster dries into a smooth seal over the mud walls.

Sun-dried bricks are made mostly of clay. For fired bricks, though, the best soil is clay mixed with sand. The sand melts when heated, then hardens when it cools. This binds the clay together strongly. Pebbles and stones,

Twisted by a giant? No, this English chimney was built with special bricks for a twisted look.

however, are a problem. These can explode when bricks are heated. They must be either removed from the clay or crushed into powder before the bricks are formed.

Builders may use bricks of different colors to create patterns and designs in the walls of buildings. Minerals in the clay used for brickmaking give the finished bricks their color. Bricks made from clay that has a lot of iron are red, reddish brown, or even pink. If the clay is low in iron but rich in lime, the bricks will be yellow or yellowish-white. By adding other minerals or dyes to their clay, brickmakers can create blue or black bricks.

Shape is another way to create unusual designs in brick. During the sixteenth and seventeenth centuries, some builders in England made chimneys on housetops using bricks that had been fired in special curved forms. When these bricks were laid together just right, they

Cement blocks, made with soil particles, are one of the most widely used building materials around the world today. They have more air in them than concrete so they are not as heavy.

created a "twisted chimney." The chimney was really straight, but it looked as if a giant had twisted it.

Another soil-based building material is the cement block. These blocks are larger than bricks. They are made from a mixture of cement with gravel and sand. Sometimes ash or small chunks of burned material is used. Blocks made from those mixtures may be called cinder blocks.

Cement blocks are made with larger soil particles than the ones used in concrete. The blocks are lighter than concrete because they contain more air. The drab gray cement block is much less fancy than a curved or colored brick. It is also much cheaper to make.

Around the world, cement blocks are used in building houses, office buildings, and outdoor walls such as the barriers along highways. They are one of the many new and old ways that people continue to use soil for building.

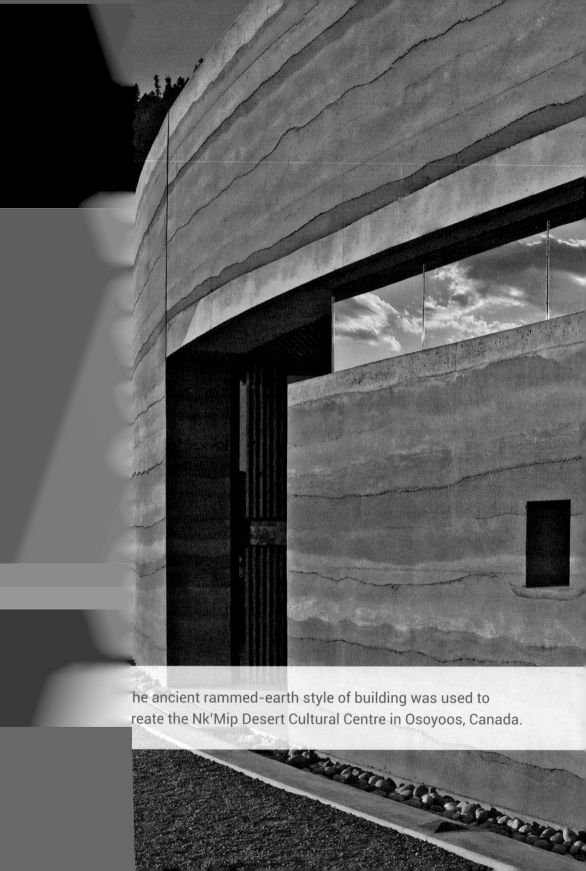

The ancient rammed-earth style of building was used to create the Nk'Mip Desert Cultural Centre in Osoyoos, Canada.

4 New Directions

At least one-third of the people in the world, maybe more, live in houses that are made at least partly of soil. That's not even counting concrete, or windows made of glass, which is sand that has been heated, melted, and then hardened in a new form.

Some people who live in **earthen** homes do not have enough money for other building materials, such as wood or stone. Often, though, people build with soil because it is tradition. It is how people have been building in that part of the world for a long time.

Why Use Soil?

There are good reasons to build with soil. The raw material for building is always handy, right under foot. It costs less than other building materials. It may even be free. Building with earth does not usually hurt the environment.

Earthen buildings are more fireproof than many other kinds of buildings. They can last for hundreds of years if they are built well and taken care of. But earthen buildings do not stand up to earthquakes as well as buildings made with wood, stone, or steel.

One of the best things about earthen buildings is the way they handle heat and cold. Soil is a good insulator. This means the insides of earthen buildings are protected from big changes in outdoor temperatures.

During winter, earthen walls and roofs hold in heat. During summer, they help the building stay cool. If days are hot but nights are cold, earthen walls soak up heat during the day and let it out at night, when it is needed.

Buildings for Earth and Beyond

People around the world are taking a new look at building with soil. They are combining old and new methods to create houses and other buildings made with earth.

One example is new rammed-earth buildings. Today, builders can buy blocks of earth already pressed until they are hard and dry. They can also use machines to press down the walls of rammed earth between the frames.

Stacking earthbags is a fast, easy, and inexpensive way to create earthen shelters.

Another new building material is the earthbag. This is a sack packed tightly with earth and sewn shut. The bags can be stacked on top of each other to make round houses like igloos.

Building with earthbags is fast and does not cost much. This type of building may soon be used to provide shelter for refugees and people who have lost their homes in disasters such as tornadoes.

Someday, buildings may be made of soil that is not from Earth. Scientists are working on robots that can gather soil from the surface of the moon or Mars, then use 3D printers to turn that soil into building blocks.

Imagine buildings made from soil standing on the moon or Mars! If that ever happens, one of humankind's oldest shelters will become our newest home in space.

adobe Building material made of earth mixed with water and sometimes straw. It can be made into bricks or poured into hollow forms of stone or wood.

cement Mixture of dry, powdered clay and limestone that has been treated with heat. Cement is used to make mortar and concrete.

clay A type of soil with the smallest grains; holds onto water and makes thick, sticky mud.

cob Mud mixed with gravel, pebbles, or small stones and used for building.

concrete A blend of cement, water, sand, and gravel.

earthen Made out of soil or earth.

erosion The wearing away of rock, soil, or other materials by wind, rain, or flowing water; one kind of weathering.

geology The scientific study of the materials that make up Earth and how they are formed.

mortar Cement mixed with water, used to hold bricks or stones in place.

mud Soil or earth mixed with water.

sand A type of soil with the largest grains; water drains through it easily.

silt Soil that is easily carried in water or air.

sod Strips or pieces of soil removed from the surface of the ground in one piece, complete with the grasses or other plants that live in them; also called turf.

soil Top layer of Earth's surface; a mix of loose earth, small rocks, gases, water, and tiny living things.

wattle-and-daub Building method that starts with a frame of sticks or poles (the wattle) and then covers it with mud (the daub).

weathering The breaking down of pieces of earth and rock into smaller pieces.

Further Information

Books

Lawrence, Ellen. *What's Soil Made Of?* New York: Bearport, 2015.

Rake, Jody S. *Soil, Silt, and Sand: Layers of the Underground.* Minneapolis, MN: Capstone, 2015.

Schuh, Mari. *Soil Basics*. Minneapolis, MN: Capstone, 2011.

Websites

Earthen Architecture: 15 of the World's Dirtiest Buildings

http://webecoist.momtastic.com/2009/02/02/earthen-architecture-natural-dirt-mud-brick-buildings/

Descriptions and examples of earth buildings around the world.

Earth Science for Kids: Soil

http://ducksters.com/science/earth_science/soil_science.php

A page of facts about soil, with links to other pages on geology, the food chain, the nitrogen cycle, and more.

Life in a Sod House

http://amhistory.si.edu/ourstory/activities/sodhouse/

A Smithsonian Institution page about sod houses on the American prairies, with photos and activities.

Index

Rebecca Stefoff has written books for young readers on many topics in science, technology, and history. She is the author of the six-volume series Great Engineering (Cavendish Square, 2015), the six-volume series Is It Science? (Cavendish Square, 2014), and the four-volume series Animal Behavior Revealed (Cavendish Square, 2014). Her books for young people have also been published by Simon & Schuster, Seven Stories Press, Oxford University Press, and others. Stefoff lives in Portland, Oregon. You can learn more about her books for young people at http://www.rebeccastefoff.com.